MW00477092

reflections

a teen's poems about navigating love
and heartbreak in the shadow of trauma,
mental illness, and a broken family

FAITH FOLEY

Legacy Book Press LLC
Davenport, Iowa

dedicated to everyone who helped to make me stronger
and got me through hard times.

also dedicated to the Family Resource Center, of which ten
percent of the profits from the sale of this book will be
donated.

TABLE OF CONTENTS

Author's & Publisher's Note

These poems address the subjects of drug abuse, mental illness including PTSD and depression, sexual abuse, and death, so they may trigger uncomfortable feelings in the reader. If you feel triggered, please reach out to a trusted adult (if you're under 18) or a trusted friend or family member (if you're over 18) for help.

The following organizations are also there to help:

National Suicide Prevention Hotline:
1-800-273-8255 or suicidepreventionhotline.org

National Alliance for Mental Health:
1-800-950-6264, nami.org,
or if in a crisis, text NAMI to 741741.

In the Quad Cities area, additional help is available through Family Resources Center.
24 Hour Free Crisis Line
(for Domestic Violence, Sexual Assault, and other violent crimes):
Illinois: (309) 797.1777
Iowa Quad Cities: (563) 326.9191
Toll Free: (866) 921.3354

mom

why aren't you here?

if you cared,
you would be here.
if you wanted me,
you would come back.

i need you.
i miss you.
but all you do is fly into the sky,
poke yourself with the needles.
the needles filled with regret,
the powder filled with danger.

why did you leave?
leave me on my own,
to grow up all alone.
hurt me and tear me to pieces,
to never try to heal me.

you gave up so easily.
you carried me.
you birthed me.
and you left me.

i say goodbye so bitterly,
as you chose dust and spoons over me,
and you continue to every single day.
as i grow up all alone,
with weights on my shoulders,
you could be here.
but you're not.

i don't

i don't remember you.
i don't remember your voice.
i don't remember your face.
i don't remember your manners.
i don't remember your sense of style.
i don't remember your laughter or tears.
but i do remember your screams,
my hurt,
my confusion,
my anger,
the scars,
the fear, along with the hundreds of tears.
i remember all of your bad and none of your good,
i don't know why but i hope it's understood.

ages of my mother

birth me when i was zero.
neglect me when i was one.
make me shy when i was two.
make me confused why i'm alone when i was three.
make me play alone all day when i was four.
teach me independence when i was five.
make me speak no sound when i was six.
give me a younger sister when i was seven.
try to buy my love when i was eight.
make me feel incapable when i was nine.
leave me when i was ten.
scar me when i was eleven.
hate you when i was twelve.
miss you when i was thirteen.
search for your warmth never to find it when i am
fourteen.

mom

you walk out the door,
leaving my heart sore.
i miss your hugs
and your sweet vanilla smell.
rides in the car with tunes in my ears,
i question if you loved me,
or if i was a mistake,
you brought me into this life,
just to bring me pain.
thanks for your lies,
along with your highs.
you've taught me hurt,
taught me fear,
but brought me strength,
made me wise.
to see through the untruthful,
see through the smiles.
it sucks that i haven't seen you in a while.
i know this is fate,
i know it's for the better.
but lately my heart has been feeling under the weather.
you're not here anymore,
and sometimes i want you to be.
i can't have you,
and that's obvious to see.
we're now different people,
changed in so many ways,
but mom, would it be the same if you stayed?

would you know my deepest thoughts?
my emotions and my fears?
would we know each other at all?
or would our relationship be bare?
i have all of these questions
left unanswered in this world.
so instead i sit here lonely,
letting my emotions fall to the floor.
as i will be put back together,
the very next day,
hide them until it's right,
cause it's only fair it be this way.

reflection of mother and daughter

the reflection of the mirror staring back at me,
glancing at my face brings me to tears.
i see you in me, and i want you to go away.
you're a part of my skin and bones,
though you are not here.
i have nightmares that i will become someone like you,
although that love and relation is sparse.
i search for you but never find you in my dreams.
but i see the resemblance on our faces.
do they see that we're alike?
do they think i'm like you?
that i'm a liar, a loser, and a cheater?
that i'm a druggie, bad mother,
and a sick human being?
or do they see me as who i am?

do we know?

the reminisce of cocaine upon your cupid's bow,
and your pupils sprout bigger than the sky,
filled with black and regret.
insert that needle of impair into your forearm,
and feel the vibrations racing through your soul,
as you can barely hold your weight onto your feet.
tumbling to the side you rumble,
you think to yourself – do they know?
do they know what – do you ask?
do we know that you're a failure?
giving in to the devils calling and letting us down?
do we know that you're gone never to be found again
sinking into the ocean of desolation?
do we know that you're hurting?
and that those opiates are the only thing
that insensate your vitality?
yes, it seems that we grasp your actuality.
you've just slipped away too far for us to care.

doll

you're just a porcelain doll,
getting others to fall at your very feet.
good perfume and pearls you make their head whirl,
now you're going to make them never want to leave.

they toss you and make your wilting body shriek,
your eyes are black, and you never feel defeat.
they do what they want and you certainly don't care,
as long as they give you a gram and get out of your hair.

your nose is so sore
from snorting that snow.
and following up you take that hell dust,
making your skin dull and never glow.

oh, how you love being played with
by all of your friends,
they give you so much candy,
to make you feel like you are ten.

once. again.

flustered

you tell me i'm like her,
by what i say.
you tell me i'll be her, if i keep acting this way.
can't you see that you make me feel weak?
can't you see that i am trying not to fall to my feet?
i am not her, in any which way!
so, stop calling me her and punishing me for what she
should pay.

i don't enjoy being screamed at,
it makes me taste defeat.
i know you feel bitter,
but you don't need to say those ignorant slurs to me.
you make me want to cry,
to question what would happen if i died,
i know you love me,
i know you care,
but if you can't control your anger,
i won't always be there.

too far gone

we were always meant to say goodbye.
the last moments of our hearts fluttering,
along with the last moment
of being satisfied in the world.
call me when it's over,
your addiction with the needles and the poison.
call me when you're sober,
i want to hear your voice when you're non-indulgent,
and see your eyes
when your pupils are not bigger than the sky.
come back when you want me,
i promise when you'll see me, you'll weep happy cries,
we'll spend hours catching up on our crappy lives.
be my mother when you're no longer a child,
playing on the playground full of candy and strangers,
with all of the lies.
but can't you see, i can't let you back into my sentience,
as you are too far gone.
you won't see me at my graduation.
you will not attend my wedding.
you will not hold my hand as i bring life into this world.
you will never be there.
as you are too far gone.

floating away

melancholy

roller coaster

up and down the view is inconsistent. you can see everything from here, while yet you can't see anything. they give you the warning signs before you hop on the ride. but you get on anyways. you buckle up, latch on, and take off, sometimes drastically, other times with the slow suspense. as you go up, the anxiety and the acceleration increases. then you plummet back down to go up once again. you're terrified, but you want to stay to finish the ride. to see how it goes, how the cart grooves into the tracks while it goes in its scheduled direction. if you have ridden that ride before, you know where it goes. you know where it ends up. people tell you when to expect all of the plummets and turns. and you still ride that ride. you still feel your stomach fall out of your abdomen. you feel your intestines twist up and your heart sink into your legs. but you want to know how it feels to ride the roller coaster of love. even if it makes you utterly and completely sick. you may fall off; you could be seriously hurt. but you take that silly chance for the thought of having that acceleration run through your veins, with a smile on your broken face.

trying

i'm trying to succeed,
forcing myself to forget,
the pain that i ever so long have breathed.
talk about lonely,
that's the description of me,
why be left alone all i do is bleed,
bleed out the insecurities inside of me.
i'm trying my best,
to leave alone the bad,
to stick on a better path,
but the wind of sighs pushes me off.
i fall to negativity,
i fall to self-doubt.
i stop trying.

head in the clouds

i've got my head in the clouds,
no time or courage to figure it out.
they may be fluffy, they may be bright,
but they are affecting my vision
on this journey through life.
don't know which road to go to,
which words to say,
the only thing that gets me through this
is the thought i'll be okay.
i'm alone and afraid with my head in the clouds,
all i need is a balloon of self-doubt to pop
so i can start to come down.

bubbles

my bubble keeps on getting popped,
the hands and hugs flooding in.
my bubble keeps on being ignored,
as i am family, a friend, or just a little kid.
my bubble keeps on getting agitated,
as it doesn't want to be touched,
it doesn't matter if it's lust or love.
let my bubble be, so inside i can be happy and free,
i want to be a bubble
who doesn't get popped and popped,
and if you won't respect that then you can get lost.

someday

i always look at the past,
getting sad about the old memories.
of when i was happy,
with the smile plastered on my innocent face.
but someday there will be better days.
someday there will be love.
someday there will be success.
someday there will be happiness.
someday. someday.
but as far as i know,
that day isn't here.
i will wait,
for someday,
to be the day.
the day someday that i am happy.

death

death is a dream,
that ever so often,
overtakes my mind,
sometimes i think about it all the time.

the last breath of a lifetime,
eyes rolling back into your head to look at your
thoughts,
your regrets,
your questions,
your memories.

lifeless in a casket,
taken by the world,
neck and wrist filled with roses and pearls.
snowy skin,
and subtle grin,
your soul was taken by the wind,
to be carried on to somewhere unknown.

death can be scary,
death can be cruel.
but death could be an escape,
from the even scarier,
crueler world.

dreams

you arrive at dusk,
engrossing me into sweet sleep.
with sweet smells of lavender and eucalyptus,
you call my name
after a prolonged day of stress and worries.
silence my words as i fall into a trance,
to dream of love that realistically never lasts.
searching for an end and reliance through the night,
flowing tears with terrors and scares,
screams and yells by innocent people.
some people wish that they weren't ever there
in that place where we go when the stars are out.
but then in a blink of an eye,
the sun rises slowly but faster than what we need.
our hopes and dreams disappear
right before we reach them,
and a new day of crushed futures
and sad thoughts begin.

fix it

shoosh,
the silence wavers the crowd.
they are finally listening now
to what you have to say.
wonder if their opinions will change
or if they will stay.
you explain yourself,
you and your demons,
and they run the other way.
damn i messed it up again.
why does it have to be this way?
i want someone to hear,
to open up their ears
and understand how i feel,
with the sadness and the tears.
but others just ignore their problems
and keep on chugging beer.
keep on popping pills.
with the needles and the fear.
i try to help myself in simple little ways,
but i can't seem to tell anybody
because they never want to stay.

puzzles of love

what is the definition of love? i know everyone ponders that same question, a record on repeat spinning in their head. well, i don't think there is a definition. love warps in ways only people on ecstasy can ever notice. everyone has different experiences with love. some are horror stories you would hate to ever deal with, some are stories you wish were your own. stories about falling in love in kindergarten, to stories of your love being brutally killed in a car accident. everyone is different, which i think is why it's so hard to find your match. it's like putting together a puzzle with pieces that came from sixteen different boxes. there are those lucky pieces that find their other piece, those pieces that think they find the one but are deceived to find out they're not. there are also those puzzle pieces that never find their match. they sit in the puzzle box all alone for eternity. more and more in this world are the people being deceived that they are ever loved. that they are ever cared for. doesn't that break your heart? they are lied to for years and years about someone they would die for. they use them and abuse them for what? just to have someone to control. to give them attention when no one else will. they make you think you're so very special, when in their eyes you're just a person to use. you don't hear about those amazing love stories much anymore. the ones where they meet in high school and spend the rest of their lives together until they are eighty. what if over time, there are none of those stories anymore? everyone is broken and is breaking others. the society will become toxic to the meaning of love. it will become an extinct thing, just like the dinosaurs years and years ago. maybe we should find our matching piece instead of tricking a circle to fit into a square. love instead of judge. let the crashing world's puzzle pieces be put naturally back into place.

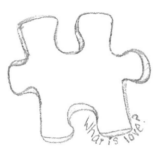

first day

ring*
they are racing down the halls,
as it's time for back to school
now that it is the fall.
everyone around me towers,
why'd they have to be so tall?
as minuscule as i am,
i feel like i'm about to explode.
make good first impressions,
make sure to hide your depression.
they treat you like you're little
while the band geeks play their fiddles.
all alone in the bathroom i'm crying
when all the others are lying.
when they say, "it gets better,"
well then why am i so freaked out?
all i want to do is sleep and pout.
endless horrors and worries,
but you got to make sure you hurry.
before you're much too late
to class on your very first day.

help me!

the children cry while the elders lie.
help me!
all you hear is the grand sighs
coming from the hurt souls.
help me!
everything is out of control
i don't want to be torn anymore.
help me!
put on the façade
of being happy till dusk when i'm alone.
help me!
i don't want to feel the pain anymore,
of being unwanted.
help me!
keep throwing those soft balls at me
"soft" doesn't mean it can't hurt.
help me!
they never understand
that one word leaves me broken for months.
help me!
i'm scared and stand alone in this world.
help me!
any hands could rip me apart at any moment.
can't you see i'm terrified?
help me!

i want it to be christmas

i want it to be christmas,
but it feels like halloween.
the haunting lights,
the pumpkins with glowing glares.

i want it to be christmas,
but it feels like eternity of darkness.
water swarming my head,
rushing in the sound of despair.

i want it to be christmas,
but i sleep soundly in the middle of june.
in the cold, lonely depths of the ocean,
tears and screams being held in my soul.

i need it to be christmas,
so people can see that i'm in fear.
so people can see that i'm too cold to speak up.
so i can finally feel okay until january.

sounds

i hear the crackling of my pepsi.
i hear the sound of the crowd.
i hear the sound of my fingers pouncing on the table.
i hear the sound of my ignorant family spewing hate.
i hear the sound of my breath
getting heavier by the second.
i hear the sound of me trying to hold back tears.
i hear the sound of my voice
breaking as i try to defend myself.
i hear the sound of me giving up.
i hear the sound of the waiter bringing our food.
i hear the sound of our dishes clanging on the table.
i hear the sound of our forks and spoons
dancing with our food.
i hear the sound of chews and swallows.
i hear the sound of my mind
spinning uncontrollably in circles.
i hear the sound of my heartbeat racing on the track.
i hear the sound of silence
as i had finally stopped listening.

roses are red...

roses are red,
violets are blue,
the traditional poems start out with you.
but little do you know roses wilt
and violets die.
not all things are pretty,
some are so devastating it makes me cry.

roses are red,
violets are blue,
not everything you hear from others is necessarily true.
some are lies, some may deceive your mind.

i don't want to hear that roses are red,
i don't want to hear that violets are blue,
i already know this, don't make me look like a fool.

tomorrow

my mind feels sunny, until it is stormy.
my heart effortlessly pumps, until it starts panicking.
my eyes are attentive, until i am no longer awake.
i am sleeping soundly,
until i am sobbing, screaming, wishing an end.
i am wishing, until i can't any longer wonder,
what it is like to be happy.
i think about happiness,
until i realize, there may never be a tomorrow.
tomorrow.
how such a game you could play with that word.
oh, what lies you could spew, with that word.
tomorrow.
they'll come back tomorrow.
you'll be fine tomorrow.
we will go tomorrow.
all of those words could possibly be true,
but they also could possibly not.
tomorrow.
it's like rolling the dice with almost all the same sides.
you never know what you'll get with tomorrow.

big kids blue

back and forth,
goes the swing on the playground.
we all grew up,
but we still think so young.
we stopped playing tag,
and instead were running from our problems.
no more playing catch with a ball,
we are now catching feelings.
this all couldn't be more real,
even though i want it to be a dream.
i wish i could go back to that park.
where everything was in its place.
the way it had seemed.

toxic friends

help

forced to grow up,
forced to lead.
i help not me but others,
even when they are mean.
even when they are pitiful,
i am right by their side,
they hurt my soul so bad i might as well cry.
but i hold back my tears,
my wishes to die.
as i am here for my friends,
even though they lie.

am I one of them?

tapping feet going down the hall.
asking myself am i one of them?
laughs, giggles, and stares,
i ask me am i one of them?
whispers and secrets behind locked doors.
i question if i am one of them.
or am i just a piece of matter?
the one who arrives but is never really there.
the thing that never gets involved,
who has her own mind and thoughts never shared?
the ignored, the rejected as i am,
i know that i am not one of them.
but i see me still asking
the same old question time and time again.
am i one of them?

hurt

i see you in my nightmares,
as well as my dreams.
your words are like nails on a chalkboard,
it makes me want to scream.
i run the other direction,
far from the hurt,
but on the way, i fall in the dirt.
tripping over my shoes,
relapsing to your warmth.
you turn cold in an instant.
leaving me frozen,
frozen in fear,
maybe that way you can see my tears.
falling down my face,
telling you to stop.
but like always,
i already know you will not.

listen

quiet is your specialist,
silence is your career.
you don't have to talk now,
no need to fear.
listen to your thoughts,
and no other living soul.
you're the only one you trust now.
don't waste your time on the old.
smiles on the surface,
grudges underneath.
your thoughts are the real you,
no need for others to preach.
preach the lies and the anger,
resentment they have,
for you will not listen.
because your good outweighs the bad.
your heart is triple the size,
bigger than most.
their negative whispers are like a ghost.
unheard, unseen.
unfamiliar to your brain.
let them drop the mike,
tumble off the stage.
the stage of rumors and drama that were made.
as you were not there,
not there to see,
the bad and hypnotic that they are made to be.

goodbye

you stabbed me in the heart,
watching me fall down to my knees.
i saw you walk away leaving me to bleed.
you search for another victim
and leave me here to die.
and i see you everywhere now,
even more then when i was by your side.
i resent your laugh,
your smile,
and the way you don't hold yourself together.
you always made up excuses,
such as "i am feeling under the weather."
excuse me, are you talking to me?
or is it the snickering and rumors i hear in my ear?
you are a hit and run accident, this time it wasn't a deer.
it used to be me that was always by your side,
but now it's those fake little girls
who are always going to lie.

control

it wraps around me like chains.
it holds me down till i drown,
and on my face suddenly appears a giant frown.
why'd you go to tie those tight ropes?
it scratches my arms.
i don't know why my crying is your favorite part.
your favorite part of this torture.
my tears, my pain.
i scream but no sound ever escapes.
i can't help myself,
so i call for others to save me from this sinking hole.
they can't hear me.
i keep falling.
attached to these chains, you have a hold of me,
for i never will be free once again.

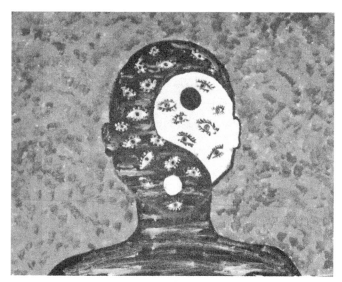

watching

PTSD

trigger warning

PTSD

it's not fair,
please don't touch my hair.
i know it's "just a hug,"
but you don't understand.
i don't touch people,
because years ago,
there were other hands.
touching my waist,
never the right place.
i'm not trying to be rude,
it just hurts too much.
to go back
in the dark, scary past.
with all of the screaming,
with all of the lies.
little do you know
your hand touching my back
always sends me back.
they never know,
my face turns like a ghost.
I shrug away the memories,
try to forget the pain,
but the PTSD will always keep me this way.

i'm ~~not~~ okay

gently soothe me
with the whispers in my ear.
all i can do is smell the beer.
traced off of your breath,
you are getting too close.
make my heart pound out of my chest.
"get away from me."
"you are scaring me," i say.
you keep decreasing the distance of our souls,
tears fall onto the pillow.
i sit still just a little.
don't want you to hurt me,
but i need to get away.
all i can do is scream,
to get your filthy hands off me.
off my young body.
you shouldn't do this to a girl.
you drink so much whiskey,
i'm surprised you don't hurl.
to this day i think back to that night,
i wish i would have put up more of a fight.

sleep paralysis

i feel stuck.
i can only move my eyes,
and my heart beats six times its size.
the man is watching me,
fingers on my thighs,
i don't feel comfortable with this, and he knows why.
i feel like i'm experiencing sleep paralysis,
feel so helpless all i can do is cry,
then i get gaslighted,
to make me feel like i shouldn't even try.
"it was just a dream" so tell me why i'm still scarred,
if anything, it was a nightmare, the worst one by far!
years later i'm still left broken,
having flashbacks of the flashlight
shining on me in the dark.
you don't realize that i'll never be the same.
you don't realize that **you** are the one
who made me this way.
i **can't** walk down the street without feeling defeat.
i **can't** be hugged or touched
without feeling that familiar pain.
can't **you** understand that i don't want to feel this way?
thank you for flipping my world upside down,
making all of the positive turn into a frown.
Such a *ray* of sunshine.

my mental illness

dealing with death

i just feel so alone. i feel like everyone is too busy. too busy with their own lives, with their own worries. nobody understands how i feel. all they see is the innocent smile that's plastered on my face when i'm around people. but nobody understands how i sit in the dark all day and don't get out of bed. nobody understands how i've cried myself to sleep for the past week and counting. nobody understands how i want to feel nothing, because my emotions are so strong and tear me down. you never realize how much someone does for you until they're gone. you never remember how much you really love them. until you can't love them anymore. until you see them in a casket soulless, hours before being lowered into the ground. the cold, empty ground. where their body's flesh and bones will wilt and rot all alone. you always took them for granted. until now. you remember all of the things they did for you. and how you will never be able to create cherish-able memories with them again. until you are dead too. you will miss their smile, their laugh, their voice. the way they look at you when you're excited, or when you just got off that crazy carnival ride with your head spinning in circles. you will remember all of the times they made your day and gave to you way more then you gave to them. you will keep on remembering them, even years and years after they are gone. you remember them because you should. after all of the things they have done. you will never forget even when you are eighty. if you even make it there. see, not everyone does. even when you couldn't imagine them keeling over any time sooner. they look so happy and healthy on the outside; they couldn't be dead in a week, could they? it always takes you by surprise. on the inside all of their organs are dying. the last time you saw them you said, "next time." well, there was no next time. you are never going to hear their voice again. you will never see their eyes light up again. you can't prepare someone for that. no matter how hard you try. and the less you try to cry, the more you want to. when you say "goodbye," you expect to see them again. little do you know that next time they are lifeless in a casket. you know their soul is with you, that they are watching over you the moment you read this, but the thought you will never see them back is the worst thing to imagine. i know you see me typing this greg. i know you want to take the pain away from all of us. i bet it tears you apart that you can't. if you were here you would give me a hug and take me out to get whatever i could possibly want. you didn't know you were going to die either. you thought about that next time too. we won't meet again for the rest of my life. and maybe even after that. i'll miss you dearly. and i know that hopey dopey will miss you and your frisbee too. maybe when hope enters heaven you can throw it for her once again.

~faith

glass

put it in the past,
i don't want to bring it back.
but everything around me
keeps me in the place where i was so scared.
and now i can't let go.
i want to relax, not always have my guard up.
i don't just work the night shift,
i'm guarding the walls of my kingdom
every. single. second.
i cry.
i twitch.
i'm messed up in this grey state of living,
everything's black and white.
glass is shattered and i'm left shaking.
trying to pick up the shards
to put myself back together.
i cut my hands and i fall onto my knees,
i'm stuck a mess as i can't seem
to put back the shards of glass into its place.
so i let my reflection shine off the pieces,
and i see my face.
with the hurt.
the tears.
the fear.

break;

i never get a break
from the grasp of evil,
drawing me into dark,
into cold,
into sadness.
i think it's over,
but it has just begun,
i should've expected this,
but i ignored it,
and now look where i am.
i'm broken.
i'm flawed,
i needed you here,
and now i don't know where you are.
all i want is a break,
from the heartache and tears,
oh god i just wish you were here.
but you're not.
and you never will be,
so it is clear to me,
and i see,
that you're gone,
and once again nothing to me.

bleeding

it all has become too much.
i'm collapsing.
the walls of strength are crumbling,
the fake smiles are turning into sighs.
for years and years i've tried to keep it together,
believe me i tried.
i'm there for everyone else but no one's here for me,
my eyes cry,
and my mouth whispers,
for help i can't receive.
the whisper turns into screams,
and my arms tremble,
as my wrist begins to bleed.
bleed the blood of the past.
bleed the blood of everything
i thought would always last.
bleed out the memories
of when you said you were sorry,
of when you said you cared.
bleeding hearts and airless sighs,
i'm draining out internally into dark,
into empty,
into cold,
i don't know if i can handle all of this anymore.

smile

lies and regret haunt me as i sit in a puddle
of my tears and memories.
of when the smile on my face was real.
true to myself, true to others.
my smile is just a shattered figure
as we're in the present.
i trick myself into thinking that smile is truthful.
when realistically it's just hollow,
inside my bones, my brain, and my heart.
slipping away by the feet goes my feelings,
tagging along my hopes and dreams.
i sit here in this world,
questioning my existence.
people say, "you got this!"
but all i have is a head full of worries,
a mouth full of red.
of the blood in my skin seeping out the edges.
i tell myself i am like the others,
but i have been misread.
listening to the monsters that swarm my head.
let me lay on my bed,
pry my eyes shut,
and hope for the best.

room

sitting in the dark,
the crisp chill down my spine,
the dryness of the air,
the silence of over a decade
haunting my consciousness.
is it okay to be this way?

no communication for hours upon hours.
the spot on the wall is my only entertainment,
the curtains with the subtle sinking light
are my company.
is it okay to stay this way?

eye circles deeper than the scars in my heart,
dry throat, from the hours
i can't grasp onto what to say.
chapped lips, deep regret,
i'm surrounded by black.
is it okay to look this way?

my heart is in my chest, only a little bit left to hold.
my head is outside of my box,
floating away to the world of empty thoughts.
my eyes are frozen,
looking into the dark and cold to never feel satisfied.
is it okay to feel this way?

i'm depressed.
and it's not your fault.
it's.
all.
mine.

lost

secrets and shame wrap their fingers
around my torn heart,
pulling at the seams till they snap.
prying the tears out of my dull eyes.
rest my head down gently over all the lies.
ignore what's coming to look at the past,
glue under my feet stuck on this path.
words will struggle till they're gone.
mind will blank and my confidence will run.
run toward the dark,
hiding from the surface,
please lord help me before they snap all my circuits.
circuits from my brain leading to my heart,
oh, can't you see that i am falling apart?
the blank that i feel during the day,
my heart sinks like an anchor.
falling like the feelings i have for life,
for love,
that will never be returned.
there's no turning back i have learned.
leaving from the good now entering the bad,
these are the mistakes i wish i never had.
now the opportunities are gone.
never coming back.
i'm sorry i have to let go of you,
but i can't stay in the past.

the face of fear

you pass through me,
flowing through my veins.
sweaty palms and intense worries,
tears running down my face.
screams escaping my mouth,
let me out of this horrid place.
running through the halls,
turning knobs on locked doors.
stepping downstairs with no destination.
my heart is beating fast, my eyes are welling up.
i can't get out of my own mind,
i'm just sitting here stuck.
stuck in a place where all of my deepest thoughts occur,
my demons hover over me telling me what to do.
i don't know how to get out since i am glued.
there's a light at the end of the tunnel,
but i can't seem to walk.
i see my happiness down there,
along with my childlike thoughts.
but my demons want me to grow-up,
something i'm not ready to be,
but i listen to my demons,
so serious i shall be.

remedy

my remedy is something unknown,
as i haven't found a cure.
to my sadness,
the emptiness i feel in my soul.
i don't want to be melancholy anymore.
i thought you were the remedy,
but damn how i was wrong.
you activate my tears,
you make the dreaded day feel so long.
i sink into my pillow at the end of the day,
i think to myself, why do i feel this way?
i want to find the remedy to my broken heart.
i don't want to pump pills into my body,
but i want to find the cure.
to my empty, hollow soul.

play dough

in the reminisce of being fourteen,
i guess you could say i am play dough.
you can toss me around and squeeze me,
to form me into something that's suitable
for your refined taste.
i discovered that around different people,
i also act different.
i don't have a defined personality.
i want to be like those other girls
who say and do what they want,
and they are loved for it.
i don't want to be a mold,
squishing myself into it around different crowds.
for example, at school i'm that sweet, quiet girl.
for example, around people younger than me,
i'm that crazy, funny girl.
for example, when i'm at church,
i'm that kindhearted, talkative girl.
for example, around my friends,
i'm that crazy and weird girl.
for example, at my house,
i'm that defined, strong, girl who protects herself.
everywhere i go i shape myself to suit your needs.
to make you happy
so i don't mess up.

leave me alone!

in the office,
telling you that "you're okay."
but you need those pills,
"don't pick up the knife,"
"i promise you, you're fine."
bills and pills piling on the table,
never enough money to afford them.
"but you need help my love,"
"before you get worse,"
"get out of bed, before you are late."
can't you see the past in my eyes,
the pain in my sighs?
i don't want to get out of bed.
i don't even want to breathe.
i'm trying so hard
can't you even see?
i'm not listening to you when you're speaking.
i'm only listening to my mind.
(don't mess up this time.)
(you have to do it right.)
(you want to take those pills, so you finally feel fine.)
two a.m. crying sessions have become a routine.
so many sleepless nights, so much stuck on my mind.
"you have nothing to worry about."
"you have so much ahead of you."
well tell me how i'm supposed to get there
if i can't even make it through
one day. one hour. one minute. one second.

i'm done with the lies of seeing people who "care."
all of you are narcissists,
only being nice to please yourself.
you don't mean all of those words,
so stop spewing them out of your mouth.
don't even hug or touch me,
i don't want to feel your warmth.
the only warmth i feel is from the hot tears
falling down my face.
when it's three in the morning and i'm all alone.
i prefer when it's cold,
so i don't have to feel.
i don't want the attention,
just **leave me alone**!
i want to be by myself and sink into my pillow.
i want to stay there and not get up until I please.
lock my door and throw away the key,
i want to distance myself from you.
so just please go away.
i'm so used to people leaving,
so i don't want you to stay.

sisterly sadness

so strong on the outside,
but you're breaking inside.
you put on that smile and spew all your lies,
deceive people into thinking you're happy
when you just want to die.
i can tell we are sisters
by the way we feel on the inside.
mine stays mostly on the surface,
while yours is mainly underneath.
you have to be the strong one
and hold me all together.
even when you are feeling sick,
so under the weather.
i've looked up to you for many years,
even through those cry baby tears.
i dropped out of my eyes
when you were
the bad guy.
but i guess we are sisters,
i guess that we fight.
but we both know,
well always be by each other's side.

good day

the sun shines down on a warm september day.
the wind ever so slightly blowing my hair in spirals.
i hear the sound of the leaves bristling,
and i see the trees swaying softly
as i walk on the track of life,
following the lines going forward.
the wind picks up.
the sun stops shining.
the subtle sound of leaves rustling turns into chaos.
i stop walking on the path and try to get into cover.
the rain starts to fall drastically,
the spirals of my hair turn into a tornado
rushing and raging into my head.
the oceans of my tears are rising,
i can't hold myself together.
the rain keeps on falling.
pitter* putter* patter*
i thought it was going to be a good day.
i thought it was going to be a good day.
i thought it was going to be a good day!

believe

the beat of the music pounds into my ears
telling me the truth by what i may hear.
i shouldn't believe what i hear,
or i shall bring on my many tears.
i shouldn't believe all i could see,
because they might be faking just trying to deceive.
i shouldn't believe all that i feel,
because it may be my mind playing chess with my heart
and at the moment making the right moves.
but later, my heart calls "checkmate"
and it takes control.
i shouldn't believe anyone or anything,
because it may all be a lie.
i should stay by myself, not by anyone's side.
all i can say is that there is no trust in this world;
it will bring many tears,
so i'll never believe what i ever see or ever hear.

bathtub

sitting in my bathtub,
wishing it would fill faster.
let it rise over my ears
because my life is a disaster.
watch the water ripple as i sit in my thoughts.
to think my life was starting to get better,
was simply distraught.
but turns out that i was caught
by the waves in the deep, dark mysterious world.
my foot is stuck on the tree branch,
i'm starting to sink down under.
this is what i wanted,
so why do i wonder?
why do i wonder what it would be like?
to not be sinking and rising enough
to just slightly stay alive?
but i'm never living.

that i'm...

i was distracted.
i went too long without feeling my burden.
i put on that smile so often i sometimes forget
that i'm bluer than the sky,
that i'm more shattered then dropped glass,
that i'm more alone then a body in a grave,
or that i'm so tired, i could hibernate
a whole winter season trapped in my head.
not dealing with my feelings
always has me sulking in bed.
so, faking it leads me to later feel dead.

toxic waste

i'm like toxic waste.
i boil and blister till i peel.
secrets and shame ooze out of my heart,
and i break down with a burning sizzle of sadness.
i can also radiate to others.
i make them rattle
with annoyance and anger,
along with concern and confusion.
nobody knows why i am so radioactive,
slipping through everything i slightly grasp
until all is
dissolved,
brittle,
broken,
shattered.
i guess it is normal for me to be so sour.
that fiery passion rushing through my head,
it overpowers anything that tries to help.
i'm left alone to figure things out on my own.
i only do this to myself.

fragments of emotion

love & heartbreak

you're sinking slowly

i don't want to feel anymore. breathing is difficult. seeing everyone around with masks and lies. haunting little children isn't a joke. pacing back and forth in the halls of captivity. the windows are boarded. the doors are locked. the key thrown into the sea. it sinks further and further, every wound letting it drop another foot. the key can't be reached. my doors can't be opened. people could cry. people will die. life isn't a joke. it should be a joke. or even better. a dream. one where you wake up and can start fresh with no consequences. see, that kind doesn't exist. happiness doesn't exist. unless you're blind to the world. to the horror. to the pain. every soul in the world has a story. all of which have a depressing scene. the earth. full of trash. the plastic kind, along with the humankind. i want to die. and so do countless others. they don't want to feel anymore. we don't want to feel anymore. we want the pain to go away. "it will get better," they say. i've been waiting for the better for thirteen years, eleven months, and twenty-five days. and it hasn't come. life should give people a break. get out of depression free card. just like the game monopoly the kids all love to play. just like the boys play with the girls' hearts. raping them of the innocence that love is a thing for everyone. that everyone has their perfect match. they pierce your lungs and heart. it throbs in your chest and sinks with the key to your happiness. by now the key is all the way at the ocean floor. it would take a miracle to find an atom of a key in the huge sea of hopelessness. many people could die trying. including yourself. the person who owns the key learned to let go. to find another way. go through another door. the door named anxiety. the door named depression. the door named hell. it leads to a future of empty gazes in your pupils. it leads to the future where that smile is forced on the little girl's face. i'm the little girl. the little girl who wants to hug her mom one last time. the girl who wants back the rose-colored glasses resting on her head before they were snatched by thieves. those evil thieves with the stupid grin and bad intentions. that little girl wants to be little again. she's still so young. holding on to so much pain and misery. why stack all this horror onto a young girl? why make this girl grow up when she's not ready? why make her take the lead and feel so much? feel so much crap that she wants to leave behind the past. feel all the things of everyone in the world, including their brother. why feel for the ones who hurt her? why feel for the ones that don't know her? why put all this weight on the girl's shoulders, letting her sink with her lucky key to the ocean bottom? drowning in all the thoughts and all the tears of the life she tried so hard to have but never received. why did you hurt the little girl? i don't think i deserved it. i don't think anyone would deserve this. but who knows because life will go on. she will smile and have the "glow" in her eyes. even if it's all a lie. she will do what she can to make them happy. even when she's terribly not.

her or me (oh when they walk away)

her or me.
a simple phrase that is used in so many ways.
but when you say that you always want them to stay.
you aren't really saying "her or me,"
you are saying "stay with me."
sometimes they leave, causing your heart to be sore
like nothing you've ever felt before.
rarely they stay, you still questioning
whether they will change their mind and walk away.
oh, when they walk away,
those footsteps pounding the other direction
is the most painful sound you could ever hear.
oh, when they walk away,
their gaze drifting as they begin to start a life
with someone new is the most painful thing to see.
oh, when they walk away,
weeks later the thought of them makes you cry;
you miss their words and affection,
the most painful thing you could ever remember.
oh, they always walk away,
leaving us permanently broken.

silhouette

i can't forget your silhouette.
i can't forget your skin.
i reach for your warmth,
just for it to be blown away by the wind.
color disappears from the sky.
tears start to well up in my eyes.
all i can see is the shadow
of what you used to be.
i see it in my dreams,
haunting over my head as i sleep.
your silhouette.
it used to be behind skin.
it used to be behind a smile.
it used to be behind ocean blue eyes.
it used to be behind you.
now all i see is your silhouette.

independence

i'm glad you're not around,
so i don't cry.
i'm happier now
because you're not by my side.
independence is my destiny,
so i'm not burned by love,
by friendship,
by family.
independence is who i am.
i don't need anybody else
to bring my sorrow-filled heart down.
i'm better alone,
so i don't get thrown around
in the tunnel of confusion and inconsistency.
i don't need to be controlled by others.
i already overly control myself.
independence is what i need,
to heal,
to love,
and try to forget.
let me be independent.
i need to forget my regrets.

butterflies

you make my head twirl
and my stomach whirl.
the butterflies will not go away,
even if i hadn't seen you in a few days.
i feel so nauseous,
food cannot compete,
i'd rather starve and be with you
than be alone and have the courage to eat.
the butterflies are hurting me,
stirring up my feelings.
my head aches,
and my eyes cry
as i miss those days where we were by each other's side.

enough

you have someone new,
you guys stick together like paper and glue.
i was never enough to you.
that girl's a diamond in the rough.
i guess i really never was enough.

in a month or two you'll be left swimming in sorrow,
not knowing if you can make it till tomorrow.
you'll be empty inside,
wondering why they left your side.
you're going to be hurt
even worse than you thought,
and you'll finally realize what you have lost.

you will finally feel how i have felt,
to lose someone you would do anything for
no matter what cards were dealt.
you will be sorry
when i'm not there.
you will be sorry
when you're alone,
so fragile and scared.

i am enough,
you're just not enough for me.
it took me months to figure it out.
now that i have solved the puzzle, i am free.
i don't have to worry about being enough.
because im alone,
and i'm enough to me.

i

i can't eat.
i can't sleep.
i can't even think.
i just want to be with you.
i need you to tell me it's okay.
i need you to tell me that i'm yours.
i want you.
i want to see your smile.
i want to hear your laugh.
i just want to be okay.
i need to eat.
i need to sleep.
but this attack of swirls in my stomach
keeps me hungry.
it keeps me awake.
i wish you were here right now,
but i may have spoken too late.

should've known

you were unavailable,
i should have stayed away.
but instead i stuck around,
and now i've got to pay.
while i was faithful,
you were not a saint.
i gave you my all,
and you just ran away.

i'm so over heartache,
i'm so over pain.
just wanted you to be happy,
but i realize you're still the same.
you broke my heart,
and i'm the one to blame.
i should've known
i was going to be played and burnt up into flames.

real

i can't tell if this is real.
i don't know if it's fake
or how i feel.
every day i'm being lured deeper in.
are we acquaintances or are we friends?
i can't tell you if it feels real,
but i can't lie and say it's not there.
why would it ever be fair?
i'm waiting for the truth to appear,
but i fear it may never reveal,
and i'll be left alone once again.

fake love

i see you slipping through my fingertips,
wonder if love ever did exist.
in my dreams i see your face,
why won't you put me in my place?
he doesn't love you,
he never will.
god, why do you hate yourself,
just swallow those pills.
make all the thoughts go away.
let the blood, the tears, and the memories
slip down the drain.
because all of this love is only in my brain.
i'll forever be alone,
so hold out on to all your lies.
damn stop lying to me,
you're making me cry.

fiddle

you strum your fingers on your fiddle,
playing such soothing music to the crowd.
you keep on playing your fiddle
as the minutes go by.
but little do they know,
i am the fiddle.
you play me every single day.
i say that isn't fair,
but you make me feel happy
when you run your fingers through my hair.
it doesn't matter
that you don't really love me
as long as you're there.
to hold me close
when i want you the most.
but in the end you're just a ghost.
you leave me like the others.
then i feel ashamed
and cry under the covers
of my california king bed.
you are still stuck in my head.

mixed feels

you mix it all up,
my feelings are stuck.
one day you love me,
the next you don't care.
this inconsistent treatment
can't ever be fair.
to my heart,
for my head,
you could be in someone else's bed.
but my mind is stuck on you.
my heart forever yours,
you decide what to do with it.
and maybe someday we can be more,
more than just "friends."
the friends who "love" each other,
but hide it from others.
is it because you're ashamed?
or do you truthfully not feel the same?
if that's the case,
stop lying to my face.
tell me the truth,
so i can deal with this pain.
and if you really love me,
be consistent and stop.
stop with the <u>constant</u> pain.

why?

why do i love you?
why do i dream of you?
why do i cry over you?
why are you a part of me?
of my heart?
i am just a piece of your day,
you are the whole entire pie.
i am just a friend,
you are my one love.
take me apart,
i will still be here.
beat up my heart,
my ears and arms will still be here,
to listen, to cuddle, to love.

betrayed

thought i had felt the worst pain,
but i discovered there is worse.
thought i was the only one,
deep down inside i knew it would never work.
put my heart on the back burner
while you tailored to others.
why'd you have to say i love you?
if you say it to ten girls.
damn you, little boy,
you make my head twirl.
just like the random girls on snapchat
who you don't even know.
say whatever you can to them
just to make them expose.
expose their bodies,
expose their souls.
can't you see i'm not like those other girls?!
i will love you!
i will cherish you!
but maybe you don't choose me
because i'm not like those other girls.
i don't show off my figure and put on a pretty smile.
i don't send pictures to boys who want their pleasure
i'm a good girl,
can't you see?
but you'll choose those nasty individuals,
over someone like me.

horrible lies!

put on a smile,
you can't see through it.
get in my way?
you better move it.
i will tear you down
if you tear me apart.
treat me like trash,
i'll treat you like that back.
even though i love you,
even though i really do care.
if your gonna look at me that way,
then mean it,
why'd you gotta stare?
break my heart and rip my soul.
didn't you learn your lesson?
you are not really in control.
don't just play around with anyone's hearts.
i'm not like those other girls.
i'm not trashy.
so don't treat me like that.
just leave already.
i can tell you're getting bored.

weight

i want to cry,
but the tears won't escape.
i really did expect this,
why did i forget that was the fate?
was ready to be betrayed,
but it took me by surprise.
i didn't know there was such evil
in those ocean blue eyes.
the anchor is sinking down into my chest.
pick off the weight before it becomes too late.
my heart is getting heavy,
the melancholy in my soul,
i thought things were getting better,
i'm not so sure anymore.

damn

i sit on that screen,
waiting for an answer.
a genuine reply.
but i find myself not getting one,
no matter how hard i try.
you will never feel the same.
you will never think the same.
as my mind that tries to grasp you
every. single. day.
make my heart burn to ashes,
my words turn into dust.
i mean nothing to you,
and i'll never know why.
i would do anything for you,
and i myself don't even know why.
why do i put myself under you?
why do i tear apart the seams of my existence,
just for you?
you take me for granted.
you don't deserve me.
but i will give myself to you anyway.

house

they fall down,
crash to the floor.
the smoke of disappointment
is smeared across the ground
in the basement of my expectations.
you built up the foundation
then picked up the sledge hammer.
there goes the morals and hope
disappearing into thin air.
the windows of love have cracks
that were caused by
the occasional hits of your fingertips.
the same ones that hold me once a week,
where everything seems right.
six other days and i'm a ghost to you.
You're still stuck on the one whom you'll never let go.
and i'm just a backup plan
for when the blueprints to your house
are lost in the abyss of this imaginary world.

flames

i play with the fire,
tossing it around in my hands
as the glow lights up my eyes,
and my pupils grow smaller
with the shine of blaze
reflecting off the pain.
i know that i can get hurt,
i could be burned to a crisp.
blacker than the mascara running down my cheeks
when it's three a.m. and i'm not holding it together.
but i still throw around the combusting embers,
taking a chance
that i'll get what i eternally want and need.
oops. i wasn't very careful.
i got charred by the coals.
and the pain strikes my nerves,
making it fall to the ground.
i forgot i was surrounded by gasoline.
the sea of flames scorches my heart,
and i cry as i realize
i shouldn't have played with your pure sparks of fire.

the same

you may like me.
you may care for me.
you might actually "love" me.
but you will never feel the same as me.
even if you do feel all those things.

i would jump in front of a freight train,
the lights blinding my vision.
the cold sweat dripping down my forehead
and the terror in my eyes.

i would sink deep down into the ocean,
the bubbles of my breath rising to the surface.
my thoughts being turned away
by the sound of inner loneliness.

i would burn in the angriest flames,
lathering my skin with embers and pain.
the screams escaping my mouth
as i turn into ashes.
being forgotten by your touch.

as you can see i'd kill myself for you
in many different ways.
i'd leave this world to help you,
and i'd stay for eternity to heal you.

i promise you don't feel the same.

"i want"

i feel the love,
and i feel all the hate.
i want to hold you so tight but i know it's getting late.
i want to scream at you and get you to realize
if you don't get your head on your shoulders
i won't stay by your side.
i want to feel your hugs,
i want you to see
how much you really mean to me.
i want to push you,
i want you to know
that you really have been hurting me lately.
but i hold it all in,
bottle up my tears, cries, and sighs.
so you'll never see how much
you're really affecting me.

addicted

i always get addicted to many different things.
i am an addict to certain foods, places, games, smells,
but most of all, i'm addicted to you.
all i thought about was you
at dawn consistently till dusk.
i was addicted to your "love."
i was addicted to your touch.
i was addicted to having someone there.
but then the other side of my complicated brain
figured out that i was actually addicted to nothing.
there was never love there.
your touch was not warming.
your gaze at me was just you observing the situation.
i now feel like a complete idiot,
forever thinking i finally could rest.
i finally could have someone care.
to love.
but then again, everyone leaves.
i'll always have to have my guard up.
i always tell myself not to let it down,
but once again i let down my walls and they came in,
with the machine guns aiming for my dear heart.

secret

i am not your secret,
so why am i kept under cover
like we weren't ever lovers?
i am not your secret,
so why am i hidden until you want to play
with my heart, my soul and my mind?
i am not your secret,
i want to be showed off.
i get that your embarrassed of me,
but then why do say you "care"?
all i want to do is show our love so bare.
but i guess i'm just a secret
you want to keep,
so hidden and neglected i will be.

wednesday

you say, "it's just lust."
and that "kids can't love."
and that may be true,
but i want to believe it's love.
but i want to believe that hole in my heart
is filled with imaginary comfort
and taken over by the gushy compliments
and soft, warm hugs.
oh, how i love wednesdays.
to see your sweet face
when i walk through those glass doors.
those two hours make my week
seem a little more whole.
i get endless affection and lovely looks
from your beautiful blue eyes.
i wish those two hours were longer,
so i could drag on the feeling of being loved.
even if it's all a lie,
something or someone to hold you over
at that place where we have a good time
when after 8:30 p.m. in the middle of the week,
we go back to our separate lives,
the lives i wished were connected more than
that one day.
wednesday.

phases of your moon

what happened to us?
where did all of the "i love you" go?
did they sink into the abyss?
disintegrated into ashes never to be put back together?
it all happened so quickly.
it happens every time.

one morning when the sun's rays
creeped onto your ocean eyes,
i was no longer your sunshine.
your feelings were always just the moon,
changing every evening
some days giving a "slice" of effort,
and others giving me your full moon.

you're still my only.
i think about how i used to gaze
at those beautiful blue eyes,
and how you can't even look at me now
long enough for me to see them.
could you tell your old self to come back?
i miss seeing him and i miss his warm hugs.
i miss that big smile, the twinkle in your eyes,
just like the midnight stars in the midnight sky.

my eyes have become not a pond but an ocean,
the waves of missing you
flowing out onto the shore of my cheeks.
i would like to think that one day you'll open your eyes
and want to come back to my side,
but your choppy words
and non-existent eye contact say otherwise.

monster

the aches and the pain,
i can't even look you in the eyes.
i wish you were still by my side.
i miss your smiles,
but i don't miss your lies.
oh, how that look on your face was so kind.
turns out you were a monster,
haunting me in my sleep.
always on my mind.
i can't help but weep.
i just need more time
to think and unwind.
to find out why.
to know why you were the beast
that feasted on my worries.
i just had to scurry
into the abyss.
oh, i think you were never the one i actually missed.

do you mean it?

do you mean it?
do you mean those delicate words?
who warp a perspective like fire?
do you mean that dangerous phrase?
that makes you look at someone never the same.
because that saying breaks and bonds people's hearts
till none longer left to juggle.
oh how "i love you" breaks my heart.

the one

it is too soon to say goodbye.
i am not ready to forget that smile.
i am not ready to walk away from my future.
i don't want to say goodbye.
but you still slip away
while i'm sleeping in midnight hour,
leaving behind your shared secrets,
the endless deep discussions, and me.
the one who was always there.
the one with the open ears.
the one who really cared.

star

i wish upon a star
as i think about how lucky you are
to not have to deal with
all the heartbreak and the sorrow
knowing that there will not be a tomorrow,
that we are together as a whole.
i feel we're connected through our souls
since the moment my eyes rose to see your smile.
oh, how i haven't seen that in a long while.
my shadow copies my heartbreak
and my actions do the same.
i didn't mean to say that to you
i guess now things will never change.

your tools

no effort was ever given,
i look like a fool.
you want to use me as your little tool.
pull me out when you want to fix your heart,
and i sit in your back pocket till
it's time to tinker your soul once again.
i'm sick of the inconsistency,
i don't want to be a tool.
i'd rather be your love,
to hold you close when you need it the most.
but i'm just a part of your collection
of your many different tools.
how i wish you used me more.
i would say i guess it is fair,
maybe you need more
than one person who "really" cares.
but i bet i'm the only one who truly wouldn't leave.
for someone else's pocket,
where they'd rather be.

hiccup

oh hiccup.
you come back in the most inconvenient times,
and you pester me for hours while i whine.
i love it once you're gone,
and i forget you till you return.
you take me off guard,
sweep me off my feet,
sometimes so quickly it begins to feel hard to breathe.
i try all the remedies to forget you,
but you keep on returning.
oh, how i hope that hiccup never comes back.

Butterflies...

the end

you've read though this book,
and you will finally know why
i cry and feel so shattered.
you can finally connect,
why i'm shy and my words don't connect but clatter.
you will see that my smile isn't how i feel,
but to fill in the emptiness inside.
you've seen that i've been consumed
into toxic humans,
and you've seen that i've been manipulated by people
i thought were by my side.
you have read that my mother has been torn apart,
and that i was invaded
by people who have no part of my heart.
you've seen all my demons,
you've read all of my fears,
don't treat me different,
because i'm still the same faith.
and i expect you to stay here.

dizzy

ABOUT THE AUTHOR

Faith Foley started writing poetry with a writing assignment in eighth grade. She began this collection in the spring of 2019 and finished it in the spring of 2020. In addition to poetry, Faith enjoys expressing her creativity through painting and drawing. She also enjoys raising chickens and playing Sims.

After high school, Faith plans to study to become an interior designer. She lives with her dad; dog, Hope; and sister, Isabel, in Iowa. Her other sisters, Maddie and Justine, also live in Iowa.